Reflections
From a Hospice Nurse

Reflections
From a Hospice Nurse

Kathy Bezinovich

Library of Congress Control Number:		2016916378
ISBN:	Hardcover	978-1-5245-4766-0
	Softcover	978-1-5245-4765-3
	eBook	978-1-5245-4764-6

Print information available on the last page.

Rev. date: 11/21/2016

To order additional copies of this book, contact:
Xlibris
1-888-795-4274
www.Xlibris.com
Orders@Xlibris.com
745989

CONTENTS

DEDICATION

I DEDICATE THIS BOOK to my sister, Claire Regina Hoffman Steckman (September 15, 1949—March 10, 1993), and to all the patients and their family members I have taken care of over the past 12 years as a hospice nurse.

"We think of our loved ones whom death has recently taken from us, those who died at this season in years past, and those whom we have drawn into our hearts with our own...
Zichronam liv'rachah
May their memories be for blessing."

DISCLAIMER

As THE AUTHOR OF THIS BOOK, I can assure you, that any of the opinions expressed here are my own and are the results of the way I interpret a particular situation and/or concept.

I would like to expressly convey to you, that were I to accidentally defame, humiliate and/or hurt someone's feelings as a result of them reading and/or acting upon any or all of the information and/or advice found in my writing, it is entirely unintentional.

In addition, all names found within my writing, have been changed with the exception of my sister, Claire.

ACKNOWLEDGEMENTS

I WANT TO THANK my dear friend, Julia Schopick, author of **Honest Medicine,** for spending endless hours editing my manuscript and advising me on the proper use of grammar and manuscript style. Without her expertise, this book would still be a rough draft. I also want to thank my husband Ned and my children Jennifer, Adam, Laura, Daniel, Holly and Nicholas, for encouraging me to turn my stories and poems into a book. Their constant love and support are greatly appreciated. And finally, I want to thank all the members of The Tamale Hut Café Writers Group, who gave me a platform to share my writing, and the support and courage to publish this book.

INTRODUCTION

WHEN I FIRST started working as a hospice nurse I had only witnessed one death—that of my sister Claire, who died in 1993 at the age of 43 of metastatic breast cancer. I became her unofficial hospice nurse because she didn't sign up with an agency until the day before she died. Because she had children, she had wanted to try more aggressive treatments before accepting the "comfort care only," provided by hospice. At the time of her death, I had been a labor and delivery nurse for ten years. Being with Claire in her final moments made me realize that, before I retired from nursing, I wanted to work with terminally ill patients. Eleven years later I left my job in labor and delivery and accepted a position as the night on-call nurse for a Chicago-based, not-for-profit hospice company.

I have never regretted the move.

Transitioning into hospice from labor and delivery was the perfect career move for me, since I felt that the shift from birth to death was the natural completion of the life cycle, bringing me full circle in the cycle of life.

There are many similarities between the two, and both require nurses to guide their patients through the various stages while using slightly different techniques. These stages are necessary to complete before the final goal of birth, or death, can be reached. Relaxation techniques, music therapy, and massage are helpful adjunctive therapies that aid the patient through both of these life cycle experiences.

There are other similarities, too: For instance, birth and death are important times in a person's life, shared only with one's most intimate friends and relatives. Also, both stages require one-to-one bedside nursing care.

Pregnant women are known to experience a sudden burst of energy prior to going into labor. Similarly, some dying people may also experience a final burst of energy and a period of clarity a day or two before their death. This burst of energy may last anywhere from a few hours to a day or two. A laboring woman experiences transition as she dilates from 7-10cm, right before she begins pushing her baby out. During transition she has her strongest contractions, which occur every three minutes, and require hard work and her total concentration. Dying people experience a transitional phase, known as "transitional restlessness," right before they enter the final "active dying stage." This stage can manifest itself with the patient tossing and turning in bed, having difficulty settling down, picking at the covers, swatting or grabbing at imaginary objects in the air, or trying to climb out of bed even though they have been bedbound for a long time. It is during this period that the dying person is letting go of her mortal life, leaving her friends and family and allowing herself to submit to death.

When I was the on-call night nurse people called me the "Night Angel" and the "Angel of Death." For obvious reasons, I preferred "Night Angel." I was often called out in the middle of the night to go into all sorts of neighborhoods to support dying patients and their families. I attended hundreds of deaths during my ten years on call at night.

Some nights, especially between the hours of 3am and 5am, I have almost fallen asleep at the wheel. I found myself in scary neighborhoods and felt very vulnerable.

But I never disliked my job.

I was not sure I would know what to say when I attended my first death, but the president of the company I worked for told me to trust my instincts and spend time listening and observing the family before trying to intervene. She said I would know what to do and say once I allowed myself to connect with the family.

Her advice was invaluable. I feel privileged to have been welcomed into so many homes where, for a brief time, I became part of a very intimate family unit experiencing a crisis. Every patient and family I dealt with made a significant imprint on my life. If I helped each patient and their family on some level, I will be content knowing my work has made their experience a little less painful.

REFLECTIONS

My job is important.

I help people achieve a peaceful, dignified death.

I provide comfort and support to the caregivers as

they perform the hardest job they will ever do;

Caring for their loved ones,

While witnessing the physical and psychological

deterioration, and end of vivaciousness.

Then, finding the courage to let go

and say their final goodbyes.

The recently bereaved are the only ones

who really know how fragile life is.

I HAVE SEEN DEATH

I have seen Death
Come in many forms.
As silently as a kitten,
Whose paws barely touch the floor.
So subtle,
That without close inspection,
One wouldn't realize,
That life has leapt away.

Like a torrid storm at sea,
Where small boats struggle
To remain upright,
As they're tossed about
On rolling waves,
Rain endlessly pouring into their hulls
Until they sink.

There are times when Death
is thrown into the ring,
for all to see.
Being down on the mat,
Wrestling with a Life not ready for defeat.

Putting up a strong fight.
Resisting the end.

Cheered on by friends
Life rallies briefly,
One more time,
Before lying down
For the final count.

The Death of a Child

WHEN A CHILD dies, it's very difficult to answer the question, "Why did God take my child so young?" There is no answer that can soothe the grieving, devastated parents. Instead, most parents try to concentrate on the positives: how their child added an element to their lives that no matter how short, was invaluable.

I once attended the death of a three-month-old baby girl, who had spent all but the last three days of her life in a hospital connected to tubes and machines. Her parents wanted to bring her home, and with the help of hospice, she was able to leave the hospital for three glorious days. For three glorious days her parents dressed her in every outfit they had bought for her or received as a gift. They photographed her in each one. She slept in her new crib, got pushed in her stroller, and rocked in her new wooden rocker. All her relatives and friends visited and held her, and had their photos taken with her. On the day she died I arrived to find the family still holding her and passing her among the grandparents for one final hug. Although the parents were sad to have lost her, they were not bitter. The mother told me she had always wanted a baby but could never get pregnant. She didn't even know she was pregnant with this child until she was in her eighth month. So, even though her daughter only lived for three short months, the mother will always be grateful and remember those three months as being her most cherished.

THE GRIEF OF A PARENT

The death of their son
Brought these two estranged parents together.
Her warm, salty tears rolled down her grief-stricken face
Dropping onto her son's body.
Their final act of bonding.
And as I left I realized
She had never stopped crying.
The Father, whose large frame filled the doorway
His head almost touching the top.
The Mother, a thin frail woman
Whose appearance revealed enormous suffering.
The Father's emotions were all bottled up,
Like a pressure cooker ready to explode.
The Mother's grief was fluid,
Like the rushing water before a rapid.
Expressing their pain differently,
Yet both were suffering equally.
When he realized his son was dead,
His grief exploded in anger,
From the top of his head
To the soles of his feet.
I could feel the energy of his rage
At losing his son.

As I maneuvered through the thick air hanging
Between him and his wife.
Throughout my visit
Her tears flowed freely and unchecked,
As she held onto her dead son's hand
And stroked his arm with her free hand.

NEXT TIME

Your voice is pinched,
Soft, hard to hear
Each clipped inhalation an effort.
You try to tell me,
I strain to hear,
And worry I will frustrate you if I ask you to repeat.
"Pardon me?" I ask,
"What were you saying?"
I want to help ease your suffering.
I focus on your needs, now, in this moment.
I hand you some pills and administer a breathing treatment.
I hope that afterwards I'll see a change.
Instead I see the fear in your eyes.
I hear you say, "I'm scared."
I acknowledge your fear,
Offer my support,
Fix you breakfast,
Your last pot of coffee,
And wish I had stayed to drink a cup with you,
Instead of saying, "Next time,"
For there will never be a
"next time."

AIR HUNGER

A condition that is frightening

A feeling of suffocation

Asifalltheairhasbeensqueezedoutofyourlungs,

Terror fills you.

I can see it in your eyes.

Afraid to move because the exertion

Brings on more suffering.

The Orange Paper

TOM CAUTIOUSLY PICKED up the bright orange sheet of paper, using his thumbs and index fingers of both hands. Holding the ends of the paper as if it were made out of a poison he did not want to touch, his hands began to tremble, causing the sheet to ripple and the dark ominous words written on it to blur. Trying hard to focus, the words, "Uniform Do-Not-Resuscitate (DNR) Advance Directive" jumped into view. Instantly he dropped the paper onto the kitchen table as if it had suddenly scorched his fingers. His brown eyes filled with tears. Gently I began to explain why he was being asked to sign the DNR form for his mother who was in the adjacent room struggling to breathe, and dying from lung cancer.

Tom looked up from the table and interrupted me.

"I know all about the DNR form," he said.

His sister, who was standing behind him, quietly added, "We don't want to talk about the DNR form."

"I apologize," I said. "I was told you wanted to ask some questions and then sign the form. But, if you don't want to discuss this now, I understand."

Several minutes of silence followed. Then Tom spoke softly, almost hesitantly. "It seems so final. If I sign the form

I feel like I am giving up on my mother. I know she's dying, but signing this form would make me feel like I was quitting."

"It's okay," I assured him. "We will still provide the same nursing and other services for your mother whether or not you sign the form. The ultimate decision rests with you since, as her power of attorney for health care, you are her decision maker. Even if you sign the form you can always tear it up. But, since it is causing you so much added stress, just put the form away and stop worrying about it. I know that taking care of your dying mother is the hardest job you will ever do. I hope you realize it is the kindest, most unselfish thing you could do for her."

I stood up and prepared to leave. Tom stood up as well and as he did the orange DNR form floated onto the floor beneath the table.

ODE TO C.H.

Death can be cruel,

Ripping through a person's gut

Like a searing pain that is

Impervious to medicines that soothe

Interested only in one thing

To fully possess and make Itself known,

Kidnapping its victim,

Without time for farewells

Without time for reflections,

Without time to fully understand that

THIS IS THE END.

The Moment of Death

I WATCHED HER DIE and felt her life force leaving her body through her fingers that were squeezing mine in a death grip. One moment she was in pain, her left leg jerking as if being shocked. Then she gestured with her arms and her eyes to her husband to help her sit up on the side of the bed. Once positioned, she became unresponsive to anything we said. Her frightened eyes looked frozen. Her husband held her left hand. She looked at me struggling to move her right hand towards me. I reached for it and was surprised by her viselike grip. Using my stethoscope I listened to her heartbeat: about the same as it had been an hour ago. Her respirations were a little faster. Suddenly, the left side of her face drooped downward. It happened so quickly I would have missed it had I not been concentrating on her.

Choking back tears her husband asked, "Is she having a stroke?"

I asked if she was a DNR or did he want me to call 911.

"No," he said tearfully. "Don't call."

A string of garbled words came out of her crooked mouth. Then she was silent. I heard her heart slow down and beat its final rhythm.

Then there was silence.

She stiffened, leaned backwards, and closed her eyes. A peaceful smile appeared where seconds before, she had tried to speak her final sentence through twisted lips.

The grief wail of her bereaved husband sounded on my right. He left the room distraught in search of his eldest daughter. I was left alone to return his wife to a dignified position in bed. I removed her catheter and medication tubing. I washed her face and combed her hair. I straightened her in the bed, placing her hands on top of the blanket. Only then could she receive her husband and her seven children, for their final farewells.

A Muslim Death

THE WOMEN WERE dressed in black from head to ankle, a scarf—type head covering wrapped in such a way as to expose only their eyes. There were at least thirty of them sitting on straight-backed folding chairs surrounding the electric hospital bed where the patient, covered with a white sheet and white blanket, lay dying, her pale face against the white pillow. The men, in white dress shirts and dark slacks, lined the hallways outside the apartment, trickling down the stairs into the warm summer night. I walked past them all, up the stairs and into the apartment, where the patient took her final breath. Almost immediately, the women began preparing her body. Hovering around the bed to form a human privacy wall, they gently bathed the dead woman and began wrapping her, mummy like, in strips of white sheets, until she was completely covered.

Special Friends

F OR SOME PEOPLE a personalized photo from a celebrity makes them feel special, as if that celebrity is really their friend. Others boast about their 1500 Facebook friends from all over the world. It is obvious that their definition of the word "friend" is very different from mine. Although all of us consider a friend to be someone with whom we share a special bond, my definition is that a friend is someone I know well enough to share my personal feelings and fears with, as well as my joyous experiences and saddest moments. My friend is someone I can trust to support me during times of need; someone who will always tell me the truth, will be available for emergencies, and will never speak against me. My friend understands when I want to be left alone, always looks out for my best interests and enjoys spending time with me even if we are just hanging out, doing nothing in particular. My friend never makes me feel obligated.

I have a hard time believing that 1500 impersonal Facebook friends are true friends. I can, however, understand how a lonely old woman might consider a celebrity who sent her a personalized photo to be a friend. I say this after meeting a patient of mine. I'll call her Doris; she was a childless widow. When she was younger and healthier, Doris had been employed in her community, had a large circle of friends, and had been very active socially. When I met Doris, she was suffering from late stages of dementia. Her small Chicago bungalow was filled with at least one hundred personalized autographed photos of celebrities. They hung in frames on the walls, and lined every available surface of her small home.

Doris's powers of attorney and primary caregivers were a gentleman and his wife, both in their fifties, who had been her neighbors for eight years before moving to the suburbs five years ago. They visited her daily, brought her groceries, paid her bills, made sure she had eaten, and took her to doctors' appointments.

On the day I met Doris, after looking around her living and dining rooms and reading all the "To Doris" inscriptions on the photos that were signed by local news celebrities, politicians, and popular crooners, I asked her caregiver about them. He told me how Doris loved to write to celebrities and ask for their photographs. Once received, she would give the photo a place of honor in her home. Her caregiver recounted stories of Doris loyally watching the early morning traffic report with Roz Varon on ABC, then talking about her as if she were a close friend. And to Doris, all these framed personalities were her friends. They kept her company during the early morning and late evening hours when she sat alone in her home, and tuned into their news or weather reports.

Now, ten years after her husband died, and with most of her friends dead or living in the suburbs, Doris never feels lonely. She enjoys sitting among her personalized autographed photos playing Frank Sinatra or Andy Williams tunes. And, during the long days that stretch on and on, since she no longer has her busy routine working outside her home, shopping or visiting her friends, Doris sits next to Oprah, Katie Couric, and Al Roker, passing the time watching other people's stories unfold on the TV and feeling content with so many friends around her.

My Dying Sister

CAUTIOUSLY I ENTERED the room. It felt too warm and there was a stale, unpleasant smell lingering in the air. The curtains were drawn, blocking out the daylight and creating a false sense of night. The air was still as I approached the bed, guided only by a dim light from the bedside lamp. The blue comforter obliterated my view of my sister, Claire, and seemed out of place considering the temperature in the room. Walking slowly across the worn Oriental rug, I went to her bed and peered over the top of the comforter. As I viewed my dying sister I felt as if I had been hit in the chest and all the air was being sucked out of my lungs. I did not recognize her. She no longer resembled my vibrant sister who had shared so many life experiences with me for forty of her forty-three years. Instead she had sunken cheeks, jaundiced skin, and was nearly bald. Her blue eyes, which had once sparkled with the excitement of life, looked glossy and stared blankly into space. Her lips, which had helped form the beautiful smile she was known for, now appeared thin and blue tinged. It was hard for me to breathe. Gasping for breath, and feeling sick to my stomach and panicky, I left the room, realizing my only sister would soon be dead.

IN MEMORY OF MY SISTER CLAIRE

Known for her trademark smile,
The musical work she did with children,
Her beautiful voice and her devotion to her family,
I meet people today who knew Claire many years ago,
And are still singing her praises.
Singing being the key ingredient to her composition.
Her soprano voice blended with many different
Chorus members.

Throughout her life she doted on her two daughters,
And involved herself in her community and her temple.
Claire started on the piano, then flute and piccolo.
She created music that brought pleasure to many.
Her talents and vast musical knowledge
Could bridge any gap and make many friends.

To Claire her family was her treble clef,
Her accomplishments the musical notes of her life.
Her marriage was her duet, her two daughters her concertos.
Like all good music Claire will always be remembered.
And like many fine musicians, because she died so young
Her life contained numerous unfinished symphonies.

A Loving Family

A FAMILY THAT TRULY loves one another is a beautiful sight to behold. I can feel their love as I enter their home. The air is still, but it is peaceful. All the adult children are working together. Their energy is focused on supporting their dying father who now lies in a hospital bed in what was once their dining room. His wife of many years sits on a cushioned chair directly behind the portable screen and makeshift curtain that is set up behind the hospital bed. Her children support her emotionally while they all await their father's death.

The hospital bed has become his throne; a dying throne. He is lovingly catered to by one or two of his daughters at all times. I watch as one of them holds his hand, and the other lifts a glass of water to his dry lips. The daughters assist me as I administer medication.

I am his hospice nurse. I have known this family for a month. From my first visit I could feel their love and concern for their father. They dote on him, watching him closely to anticipate his every need. At first he would talk to them, but today he is silent, a step closer to his final journey. He does not look afraid, just tired.

During my first visit we were able to communicate verbally. I assured him that I would do my best to support him and his family and do whatever was necessary to eliminate his nausea and pain.

I have kept my promises. He is resting quietly without pain. His body is ready to die, but his soul hesitates because his family does not want to let him go. He will hold on for a few more days. I will help the family find the courage to let go and say their final goodbyes, so they can perform their final acts of love.

The Human Will to Live or Die

UNTIL I HAD worked as a hospice nurse for several years, I didn't realize the true strength of the human will. I am talking about the will to live and the will to die.

I once took care of an 89-year-old woman—I'll call her Mary—with metastatic cancer of the stomach. She resided in an independent living facility in Chicago. Her prognosis was three to six months, and she was just beginning to feel pain. She lived independently and was alert and oriented to person, place and time. She had run several businesses, and was comfortable making important decisions and calling the shots. She had two daughters who did not get along with each other. One lived in Chicago and the other, in Los Angeles.

Mary met with the people from hospice and said she wanted to sign up. Although she was beginning to have some pain, she would not agree to start taking any morphine until after her California daughter visited to help her go through her closets and organize her papers. Consents were signed on a Monday, and her daughter arrived on Tuesday and stayed until the following Monday. During this time, Mary took care of all her personal business, cleaned out her closets and had her daughter write down where each of her items should go after her death. After her daughter returned to California, she called her Chicago daughter over, and they said their final farewells. The very next day she said she was ready to die and wanted to be started on morphine. She asked for a nurse to visit her at 6am to administer her first dose.

When I arrived Mary told me she was ready to die, and said she knew it would happen in a day or two. Still new in my job I told her we could never know exactly how much time we have left to live, but she calmly disagreed and said she knew. Twenty-four hours later she took her last breath and died peacefully in her own bed. I realized then that she had been able to will herself to die quickly.

The opposite scenario has occurred with several of my patients. Their will to remain alive is so strong that despite their terminal diagnoses and their emaciated, almost skeletal bodies, they manage to outlive their predicted death by weeks or months.

At 84, W.T. had a will to stay alive that was stronger than the natural deterioration and wasting away of his body. It must have been his feisty nature that kept him alive so long. W.T. would assert his rights as a vet, trying to claim everything he was entitled to during each of my visits. His siblings and children all lived out of state. He lost his independence first, then his endurance, and last, his appetite. And through all these physical changes, W.T. retained his feisty personality and his memory. His mind was still sharp enough to recall the phone numbers of his most important relatives. He lost over 35 pounds and needed help with all his activities of daily living. He became bedbound and totally dependent. His active dying stage went on longer than any other patient I had encountered. I knew his will to live was the only thing keeping him alive. Every day I would check my messages anticipating that his name would be listed as someone who had died during the night. Weeks passed and although he looked emaciated and was unable to eat more than a tablespoon of food or a few sips of Ensure, he remained alive. The last time

I saw him alive, he had that glassy-eyed look as he stared up toward the ceiling and reached in the same direction with his outstretched arm. Finally, on December 31, the last day of 2015, W.T. took his final breath and succumbed to death.

Peaches

A S SOON AS the paramedics entered the bedroom, Tom awoke with a start. He felt confused and frightened as he watched the three paramedics hover over the twin bed on the other side of the room where his wife Priscilla slept. They were hooking her up to a machine as they spoke in muffled voices.

He became aware of the other people squeezed inside the doorway. Mary and Denise, the two night nurse's aides, stood shoulder to shoulder and behind them was George, the night desk clerk.

Denise walked over to Tom and said, "I'm so sorry. Priscilla was so animated and talkative with us last night before bed. We were both shocked to find her this way during our nightly rounds. We'll help you contact your son after the paramedics leave."

Then it suddenly hit Tom. Priscilla must have died in her sleep.

Suddenly one of the paramedics turned toward Tom and said, "I'm so sorry for your loss, Sir."

"My loss?" Tom replied as a question. Tom climbed out of his bed and moved toward Priscilla's bed. The paramedics had removed the EKG leads and were lifting her onto the gurney. Tom reached for Priscilla's left hand. It already felt cold. Carefully he twisted off the plain gold wedding band from her ring finger that he had placed there 60 years ago. The nurse's aides surrounded him. Mary, the youngest, was crying softly.

Tom managed to walk over to the doorway and block it before the paramedics wheeled Priscilla out of the bedroom. He bent down and gently touched her cheek, first pushing aside the few stray gray locks of hair that always seemed to fall across her round face. He kissed her quickly, one last time, and whispered so no one else could hear. "Rest in peace, Peaches." That had been his pet name for her during their life together.

He had called her Peaches because she had always been "pleasantly plump" and had a peaches-and-cream complexion. She always had a sweet personality, and never raised her voice at anyone. Priscilla had been a kind and patient mother to their one son, a loving and devoted wife, and had spent 30 years working in the public school as a beloved kindergarten teacher. Last week she and Tom had celebrated their 60th wedding anniversary. The executive director of the assisted living facility where they lived had offered to pay for a haircut and style at the facility's salon, but Priscilla had refused. Her once thick curly blonde hair had long ago thinned out and turned gray and stringy. Tom barely noticed. He was unaware of the number of residents who complained to the director of the facility about Priscilla's unsavory appearance and odor. Intellectually Tom knew that Priscilla suffered from early dementia. He knew she had never felt compelled to dress up for others. There had been more than one meeting with the director, the social worker, and the nurse of the facility during which they strongly encouraged him to convince Priscilla to go to the salon to get her hair washed, cut and styled, and to allow the nurse's aides to help her with a daily shower. Tom never gave in to their requests because he felt it was important for him to support his wife in her wishes to remain independent as long as possible.

For their 60th anniversary they had eaten a specially prepared dinner in the dining room. Seated by the windows on the 13th floor, they had a beautiful view of the Chicago skyline at night while they ate and held hands. When Tom stared into Priscilla's eyes, he was unaware of anything displeasing about her. Instead he saw Peaches exactly as she had been 60 years ago on their wedding day.

A First Year Reflection

D URING MY FIRST year as a hospice nurse I found myself in an uncomfortable position while attending a death call. I was a novice at attending deaths since I had only been present at a handful of them, and was still on a learning curve as far as how to deal with difficult situations. I knew there was a social worker on call during the night available to me if I needed her help, but I had not called on her too often.

The patient was a young man, around 45 years old, who lived with his mother. He had died around midnight, and when I arrived, about an hour later, his mother was devastated, and trying not to acknowledge that he was truly gone, was sitting on the bed where he had died, holding his hand.

As I entered the bedroom she asked me to double check to see if he was dead. She thought she had seen some movement. The patient was lying on a regular double bed on his side. I placed my stethoscope on his chest and listened for a minute. No heartbeat. I placed my fingers over his carotid, and not feeling a pulse, confirmed that he was definitely dead. I told his mother. She started crying and said she would not leave his side.

No funeral plans had been made or even thought about. I went in search of his three siblings who had gathered together in the living room, and found them surrounding a coffee table covered with empty beer cans and wine bottles. The eldest brother was searching in the liquor cabinet for what he referred to as "the good stuff." The clock on the wall indicated that it was 1:15am. I needed to get this family to pick out a funeral home before they all drank too much to think. I needed help. I remembered the conversation I had with the night social worker, when we met for dinner shortly after I had started. "Call me anytime you need my help at night, no matter what time." I snuck off to the bathroom and locked the door. Once the door was secure I dialed her number.

Our social worker answered and I said, "I need your help. I'm at a death and I've locked myself in the bathroom while the family is pulling out bottles of scotch and whiskey in the living room. The patient's mother won't let go of the body, and no one has thought about any funeral arrangements. I'm worried that I will be stuck here all night waiting for the family to sober up enough to choose a funeral home."

She assured me that she would call the family on their house phone, and obtain the name of a funeral home, then call me back. I thanked her and left the sanctuary of the bathroom. Once outside, I ventured back to the bedroom where the patient's mother was still sitting on the side of the bed with her arms around her dead son's body.

I told her I would clean him up and prepare him for the funeral home. When I rolled him over onto his back, a low moan escaped his lips. Shocked, I looked up at the mother to see if she had heard the sound, too. Luckily for me, she had stood up and walked to the bathroom so she hadn't heard anything. I hastily checked for a pulse again, and reassured that there was none, and that the moan was just a release of internal gasses, I continued my job of cleaning and dressing the body. By the time I finished, our social worker had called back and provided me with the name and number of the funeral home the family had chosen.

Despite the enormous amount of alcohol the siblings had consumed, they all gathered around their brother's body to say their final farewells. They stood beside their mother and embraced her, each sibling helping to support one another and their mother. When the funeral home arrived, they were able to pick up the body and transfer him to their cart with dignity and in peace.

Old Men Are Easily Forgotten

A S I SIT by your bed, holding your hand, I recall our first meeting ten months ago. You were living in your own house then, taking care of yourself, going out in the neighborhood, visiting friends and relatives. There were always relatives stopping by. Sometimes they would help you out by driving you to the store or the bank. Sometimes they would buy you food. Your grandchildren and great grandchildren would visit and bring you laughter. The smallest ones loved to play at your feet and share your food. Whenever they were around, your eyes would light up and you would have a smile on your face.

Slowly, you started losing your independence. You needed to use a walker when you went out in case you became too tired or too weak to stand, and to help you maintain your stability while walking. When you returned from your outings, you needed a long nap to be able to function. You still lived alone and kept up with your household responsibilities. During this time you spoke fondly of your grandchildren, and how you supported them through school, helped them buy cars, and offered them refuge in your home when they needed a place to stay. On more than one visit I saw you handing one of them a wad of bills.

Eventually you needed more help and arrangements were made for a homemaker to come for four hours a day, five days a week. Your prickly personality resulted in going through quite a few different homemakers before finding one or two you liked well enough to not dismiss after their first day.

Then, even with the homemakers coming five days a week for four hours a day, and our hospice nurse's aides coming in daily for another hour, you needed help 24 hours a day. Your granddaughter and her babies moved in and offered to help take care of you. But she would leave you alone for long periods of time, and you needed to maintain your dignity and carry on with your personal business. You couldn't wait around until she decided to return. So, one day you ventured out by yourself to buy something to eat. Unfortunately, you didn't realize just how weak you had become. Luckily you had your cell phone in your pocket and were able to call for help when you fell crossing the alley near your house. The police arrived and the paramedics took you to the hospital. Nothing was broken so you were sent back home, and your granddaughter promised to be more accountable. She kept her promise until the 4th of July when we had temperatures in the upper 90s. That evening she went out to see the fireworks and left you alone. Your neighbors called the police when they heard you banging on the window yelling for help.

This time the hospital social worker and medical staff decided that you needed to live in a nursing home where you would have 24-hour care. At first it seemed like a good idea to you. But soon you realized that visitors were sparse, and then nonexistent. No one kept in touch. Your phone was confiscated by the staff after you called 911 several times saying you had been kidnapped and wanted to go home.

And where was your family during all this time? Without your physical presence around, it seems they had forgotten you. Your son and daughter both live in the south. They both work full-time, and said it just wasn't a good time for them to take you into their homes to care for you. They were relieved to hear you were placed in a nursing home. Your daughter and son have each visited a few times, and have spoken to you over the phone. Your granddaughter and niece visited once or twice, then disappeared. Your granddaughter and her children are now squatting in your home.

When we first met, you were feisty. Every week you demanded your rights, your VA benefits, and fought to get as much assistance as you could. I would leave your house hearing your favorite phrase in my head: "I'm 84 years old, and a veteran, and after serving my country, I have earned the right to have my needs taken care of!"

I know you like your coffee and foods hot, not the way they are delivered to you in the nursing home. You also like a warm home, with extra blankets on the bed, and no air conditioning, unlike the environment in the nursing home. There you are always complaining about feeling cold. And now that you are bed bound, you are totally dependent on others taking care of your every need. How can you maintain your dignity when you need someone to clean you up after you've defecated in your adult diaper? What is even worse is when there is no one around to do this job and you have to lie in your own waste until someone shows up.

Your face is so thin you would look like a skeleton if you didn't still have a full head of fuzzy white hair. You have lost so much weight that even the small diapers are too big for you. Today you took a few sips of the coffee I brought, then managed a weak request to be turned over on your side. Even turning yourself is impossible without help. Your body is shutting down. You manage only a few bites of food per meal, and a few sips of liquid. It is even too exhausting for you to speak. I hold your hand, wrapping my warm fingers around your long cold boney fingers. You close your eyes and surrender to sleep, waiting for death.

Designer Death

C HICAGO'S GOLD COAST officially got its name at the turn of the century because of the number of wealthy Chicagoans living there. At the time it was the second most affluent neighborhood in the U.S. The Gold Coast covers the areas between North Avenue, Lake Shore Drive, Oak Street and Clark Street. It was here, in one of the more elegant condominium buildings, that I encountered my only "designer death."

The widow barely spoke as she ushered me into the lavish bedroom decorated in muted colors. Her recently deceased husband lay on top of the mauve satin comforter. She was dry-eyed and spoke in a whisper.

"I want you to dress my husband in a special outfit before the cremation society picks him up."

She handed me a neatly folded pile of clothes.

"The shoes are in the box, and when the people come to take him away, be sure you hand them this box and instruct them to place his ashes here before returning him to me."

She handed me an elegant gold embossed Gucci shoe box, turned abruptly without giving me time to ask any questions, and exited the room, closing the door behind her.

I sorted the clothes in the order that I would need for dressing the body. Underwear, pants, undershirt, socks, sweat pants, polo shirt and matching sweatshirt, all the color of caramel candy, and each piece ultra-soft to the touch. Every item bore a designer label.

I placed protective sheets around the body on top of the satin bedspread, removed the pillow from under his head, and placed it on the chair. I knew that being neat and preventing any bodily fluids from spilling onto the expensive satin bedspread would be important to help this patient maintain his dignity through this final act.

Candy Bars and Conversations

I HAD A 63-YEAR-OLD colon cancer patient, whom I will call James. He was a resident in a nursing home. I was told that he had been homeless and living on the street prior to coming to this nursing home. It was not my favorite nursing home, but it was not the worst, either. Unfortunately, it seemed to be the nursing home on the west side of Chicago where large numbers of homeless mentally ill patients were placed. James was not mentally ill, but he was placed on a floor where it seemed that one third of the patients were mentally ill, another third had dementia, and the last third had a variety of health problems. Most of the residents were wheelchair bound. During the time James lived there, he occupied several different rooms. Each one held three patients. James was always the youngest in the room and the most alert and oriented. He told our social worker that he had no family, and gave us the name of a friend with whom he had stayed for short periods of time, but was not his power of attorney. James was "decisional," a legal term meaning that he was able to make his own decisions.

By the time he became our hospice patient, James was bedbound. He could no longer stand or support his weight. He spent his days watching TV. He had wild, unruly brown hair that was streaked with gray. He also had a wild-looking beard. I visited James weekly, and each time I would try to engage him in conversation, but James was not much of a talker. For the first month he would refuse to let me take his vital signs, but he was always polite, saying, "Next time." He just didn't want to be bothered. I also think since he had lost control of everything else in his life, saying no to me was the last piece of control he had left.

When Christmas came around I baked cookies and brought them to several of my patients. James really enjoyed my cookies and that day he spent a few minutes talking to me about something he had seen on the news. At my next visit I brought him a candy bar, and he told me his favorite candy was Fast Break, so I promised to bring him one next time. Thus began our candy-and-conversation relationship. I stayed for the time it took him to devour the candy, and during that time, James would converse with me. I realized that the bigger the candy bar, the more time I could spend with him. I searched for the giant-sized bars, and always arrived with one or two.

During one of our visits James started talking about Las Vegas. He must have spent about thirty minutes telling me how, a long time ago, he went with a friend to Las Vegas and they stayed there for several months on very little money, by taking advantage of all the cheap food, freebies, and complimentary rooms available when you spent enough time gambling in the casinos.

After that visit, he started letting me take his vital signs, which I would do before giving him his candy bar. I would ask him if he had any other wishes I could help him with. He always said no, that he did not want or need anything else. I would encourage him to allow the male nurse's aide to help him shower, and wash his hair and give him a shave. He finally allowed him to do that, but only once a week, and he never let anyone cut his hair or trim his beard.

One day I arrived with a candy bar and he asked me to put it in his drawer. The week before I had brought him some Hershey's Kisses, and they were still in his drawer. I knew this was an ominous sign.

The social worker had been talking with him since the beginning to decide what he wanted to do with his body at the time of death. He said he didn't care, that he had no life insurance, and there was no one he could ask to help him out. The social worker suggested body donation, but James refused. On the day James died, his body was transported to the city morgue.

I thought this was the end of James' story until a couple of months later I received a call from someone claiming to be his daughter. She said her mother had received a letter from the morgue. Even though James had changed his last name slightly, the morgue had tracked his ex-wife down from their marriage license. Her mom and James had been married, but when she was eight years old and her sister was two, James had left them and hadn't stayed in touch. The last time they heard about him, he had been living in Las Vegas. She told me her mother was going to claim his body, pay the storage fee, and then they were going to have him cremated. They were also going to have a simple memorial for him. She asked me to tell her as much as I could about James since she barely remembered him. She wanted to know what he had looked like. She enjoyed hearing my stories about his love of candy bars. I told her he had been a quiet man who did not talk much, but was always polite. I told her that during one visit he fondly recalled the time he lived in Las Vegas.

If his family had not stepped in to claim his body, James would have been buried in an unmarked mass grave with other unclaimed, unwanted bodies. I was happy for James that he was reunited with his family and would have a dignified ending to his life.

Frozen in Time

THE PHOTOGRAPHS ON the wall portrayed a vibrant, pretty woman happily interacting with various friends, family members and especially her husband and small son. In the photos her child matured from about five to ten years old. There were family parties, vacations at the beach and on a cruise ship, and photographs of Joan generally enjoying life. I searched the walls for more of her life story, and found none. Her family life was frozen at age fifty, the age at which she was diagnosed with early onset Alzheimer's disease.

Further inquiry concerning her son's age and current whereabouts resulted in learning that he chose not to visit his mother anymore. He did not want to acknowledge the woman she had become; the woman whose life had been trapped by this disease. Instead, he preferred to rely on his memories when he was ten and when his mother had been entirely present, and whole. Even her sisters rarely visited or called to check on her. Life for Joan had narrowed down to the company of her husband, the healthcare workers who looked after her, and all the pictures displayed on her walls, of how she had been before she lost control of her life.

The People Who Live Inside

THE CITY OF Chicago contains buildings with a variety of architectural designs. As a hospice nurse who makes home visits, I have been privileged to have seen the insides of many different types of architecture. The south side of Chicago with the Pullman area, Hyde Park and its many examples of Art Deco, downtown with examples of Mies van der Rohe, and Oak Park and River Forest with many Frank Lloyd Wright, and other Prairie style homes. There are also the amazing new high rises downtown with fabulous views of the lake, Centennial Park, or the Buckingham Fountain. I always take note of the fine details, the art glass or leaded glass, the beveled mirrors and inlaid hardwood floors. Paneled and sliding doors and 12 foot ceilings adorn others. Many homes are a mixture of preserved old exterior architecture, with the most modern, sophisticated kitchens and bathrooms. I have walked among delicate antiques, and have seen rooms full of priceless furnishings and artwork.

Driving around Chicago, I can go through most neighborhoods and recognize certain buildings which remind me of the different patients I have cared for who lived inside. In Lincoln Park, there was an old woman who had died in one of the very expensive brownstones on Orchard Street. She had been a famous choral conductor and pianist. Her Steinway grand piano occupied half of her narrow living room. While I was preparing her body for the funeral home, her caregiver told me all about my patient's musical career, then played a recording of her performing several piano sonatas. Listening to her play transformed her for me from a stranger into someone who had spent her life creating beautiful music that she shared with others.

One Art Deco building across from Lincoln Park had an enormous marble entry hall. The patient who died in that building had been a famous dancer and choreographer. His guardians, who greeted me, told me that when he had been younger and healthier, he had performed yearly in the marble entry hall for the residents and their special guests. Upstairs on the wall above where his hospital bed was placed, was a hand-painted mural depicting the patient dancing on stage with Fred Astaire.

In another Art Deco building, this one in Hyde Park, I met a patient who lived in an 11-room condo. There were French doors between the dining and living rooms, several fireplaces, hardwood floors throughout, and many pieces of antique furniture. This patient had performed as a famous ballerina of a leading Chicago ballet company. After her performance career ended, she spent many more years teaching others how to dance. Her pink toe shoes hung from a special hook on the wall in her bedroom where she now spent most of her time lying in bed.

I have had several patients who lived among their art collections that covered every available wall space, turning their homes into art galleries. I remember the inside of one home in particular. This patient had taken a very large open space with basically no full walls, and divided the space into many smaller areas, on several different levels, giving the appearance of small islands. Each island served a different purpose. One was designated the living room, one the kitchen, one the dining area, one the sitting room, and one the bedroom. Different styles of art covered the walls. Each island was on a different level separated by several steps. This design created a unique, although somewhat overwhelming, art gallery to be viewed from several different angles and levels. Unfortunately for this patient, when she became unable to walk up and down stairs, her bedroom literally became her island.

I have walked through homes in various historic districts: in the Gold Coast, the Pullman District, Lincoln Park, Hyde Park, Oak Park, River Forest, and in the best and worst parts of the West and South sides of Chicago. I discovered that there is beauty to be found in all of these locations, although you often have to look past the clutter and decay to see the original splendor of the buildings.

Several Silhouettes

I HAVE MET SO many fascinating people while working as a hospice nurse. Unfortunately, by the time I meet my patients, many of them have deteriorated so much that I can only catch glimpses of their true pre-illness selves. Often it's from a brief conversation on a particularly lucid day, a long conversation with a family member while doing a life review of their loved one, or by taking note of my patient's personal belongings, including photos, memorabilia on shelves and walls, and book collections. I learn the most about my patients from these observations.

I always study my patients' homes for special details about their lives. A wall, a dresser, or a mantle covered with family photos indicates how important family is to them. I can often tell something about them from their collections. I have seen kitchens where the wallpaper, place mats, salt and pepper shakers, and dish towels were decorated in unique ways. The themes ranged from Pillsbury Doughboys and Doughgirls, cows, roosters, pigs, sunflowers, and Disney characters. One of my octogenarian patients displayed her many bowling trophies on her mantle with plaques recording her scores and championship titles, some as recent as the previous year. A home with walls lined with books usually indicated the patient had been a professor, teacher or researcher. One patient had the largest collection of penguin figurines I had ever seen, made out of various types of materials including glass and wood. This patient's small, one- bedroom apartment had floor-to-ceiling, wall-to-wall bookshelves in the living room covered with penguins. Another patient collected old cameras. When she moved in with her daughter, her daughter installed a shelf 12 inches below the ceiling that went all around the room. All her cameras were displayed on those shelves, and when she was in bed she could look up and see them all.

Salt and Pepper Shakers

W.S. was 79 and during the last 40 years of her life she collected salt and pepper shakers. This was one of my favorite collections. When I sat at her dining room table with her daughter, I was surrounded by four china cabinets, each filled with many unusual and unique salt and pepper shakers. Her daughter told me that W.S. loved to travel and each time she went somewhere new, she would visit their secondhand shops and gift shops, in hopes of finding a new piece for her collection. She would also often go to flea markets or garage sales to purchase salt and pepper shakers. Besides having a salt and pepper shaker for every official holiday, she had shakers decorated with various kinds of animals, as well as celebrities, like Marilyn Monroe and Charlie Chaplin. I also noticed an entire shelf filled with various Disney characters made into salt and pepper shakers. Her daughter sadly confided that, after her mother's death, she wouldn't have room in her house to display the entire collection. We discussed the possibility of giving a salt and pepper shaker set away to each person who attends her mother's funeral.

Twelve years of visiting hospice patients and hearing them tell me about their favorite foods has led me to associate certain foods with particular patients.

Jelly Beans

I took care of one patient for almost a year, who has forever changed the way I feel about jelly beans. Ninety-three-year-old Nell had loved jelly beans since she was a young child. She would ask for a jelly bean from the moment she awoke, until she went to bed. Even though she would say, "I want a jelly bean. Please give me a jelly bean," she always expected you to place two jelly beans in her mouth. For years her family kept a small dish of jelly beans at her side. Each time her request was granted, she was sincerely grateful.

The day she stopped asking for her jelly beans, I knew Nell had begun her transition. Her family acknowledged this change and prepared for her final moments on earth. When she died and was regally laid out for all her friends and relatives to pay their final respects, it was only natural for a bag of jelly beans to be placed inside her casket to accompany Nell on her final journey.

Peppermint Candies

Georgia loved red and white hard peppermint candies. She had about ten candy dishes in her living room and every one of them was filled to the brim with peppermint candies. She told me that her friends and family always associated her with these candies. Since then I cannot look at a red and white peppermint candy without remembering Georgia.

M & M's and Tootsie Rolls

William fought a long battle with his cancer diagnosis .He loved M&M's and Tootsie Rolls. When he became confined to his bed, his wife made sure he always had a jar of M&M's at the bedside, as well as a big bag of Tootsie Rolls. On some days he wasn't able to fall asleep, and his wife was convinced it was because of all the caffeine he had ingested from the M&M's and Tootsie Rolls during the day. But, realizing his only view of life was limited to the angle he could see while lying on his back in bed, and understanding the amount of pleasure he had from these candies, his wife couldn't justify restricting his consumption of this caffeine-infused sweet treat. Therefore, William enjoyed these two candies until the day he could no longer swallow.

Egg McMuffin

For another hospice patient who had been living in a nursing home for most of his adult life, a one-day-a-week ritual was established where I brought him an Egg McMuffin and a medium coffee from McDonald's. Michael seemed to look forward to our visits and allowed me to evaluate his health and review his current medications while he ate his breakfast.

Fruit Smoothies

Roxanne lived in the basement of her mother-in-law's home. Her two roommates were her husband, when he was not traveling for his job, and her Pitbull , Mellow. Mellow lived in a large crate that was located arm's length from Roxanne's hospital bed. As soon as I began knocking on the door, Mellow would start growling, a soft throaty growl that would work its way up into a loud full growl/bark combo which sounded like he was hungry and smelled a tasty dinner approaching. Until I heard the "all clear" from Roxanne, I would not stop leaning against the outside door. Then I would slowly push the door open. Three weeks before Roxanne died, she started craving fruit smoothies, so I would stop off at Dunkin Donuts to buy her one before visiting. I am happy to stop thinking about that growly Pitbull named Mellow, but I will never be able to pass a Dunkin Donuts without thinking about Roxanne.

Taco Night

Leslie was only 31, yet her life was ending. She had a brain tumor and was dying. She had just celebrated her first wedding anniversary with her husband in the house they had bought together right before they got married. Her wedding picture hung on the wall behind her extra-large hospital bed. The girl in the photograph had long, wavy hair, a beautiful smile, and pretty blue eyes. The girl in the bed was bald, and weighed at least 100 pounds more than the bride in the photo. Massive doses of prednisone and other steroids were responsible for the extra pounds. Chemo and surgery had removed all the beautiful locks of hair. Yet despite the way the drugs had ravaged her body and distorted her appearance, her pretty blue eyes and beautiful smile remained. During the short time I took care of Leslie, she always remained positive. She lived each moment to the fullest, and never seemed to dwell on the past, or obsess over her lack of a future.

On one Tuesday visit, Leslie's best friend was in the kitchen cooking up a Mexican feast. Two certified nursing assistants from my hospice company were giving her a bed bath, and we all helped apply lotion to her skin to help soothe her constant itchiness. The spicy aromas and sound of onions sizzling in the next room led me to inquire about the Mexican feast that was being whipped up in the kitchen. Leslie told me it was Taco Tuesday, when her girlfriends would come over after work and they would all eat tacos and drink Margaritas together.

Having just finished her bed bath, Leslie, from the waist up, was nude under her covers. She rarely wore anything besides an adult diaper, because most clothing irritated her skin. I asked her where I could find something she wanted to wear for her party. She looked me squarely in the eyes and said, "I don't need you to get me anything to wear. Everyone knows it's Topless Tuesday Taco Night, when tops are optional. My girlfriends are comfortable with the arrangement, and some might even join me."

In Conclusion

I HAVE BEEN WORKING as a hospice nurse for twelve years, and during that time, whenever anyone would ask me what kind of nursing I do, and I'd answer by saying "hospice nursing," their immediate response, almost every time, would be, "It takes a special kind of person to work hospice. Isn't it difficult to work in such a sad area of nursing? You are doing God's work."

My answer is always "Yes, it does take a special kind of person to work in hospice." Not everyone is cut out to do this kind of work. It's a job that can only be done by a person who is sincerely interested in hearing what her patients and their family members are trying to say; otherwise, there will be no true communication. If you are the least bit insincere, or indifferent, you have no business being a hospice nurse.

An unskilled listener may not realize that the first few things a dying patient or family member says, may not be what he or she really wants to talk about. During your first encounter, they may just need to vent their most recent emotions before saying what is really on their mind. You must acknowledge these feelings and give them space to open up. Take a step back and listen. They may not be willing to talk or open up during this first meeting, so you must be willing to accept this, and offer any necessary information with compassion and patience. If you continue to listen with an open mind and heart, they may soon decide to share more information and emotions with you.

I have learned that when people are feeling a great deal of anger, sadness, frustration or disappointment, these emotions must be released before they are able to have an honest conversation. As their hospice nurse you must make it clear that anything they say is confidential and that they are safe to express any thoughts and emotions with you. Remain objective and don't try to change their minds or tell them they are wrong. Simply acknowledge that what they say is true, and express only your sincere regrets and sympathies.

On many occasions a patient or family member has lashed out at me with anger. This anger is usually about a situation neither you nor they have any control over. The dying person is usually angry about losing control of their life and not having any other options. This is the saddest part of being a hospice nurse, watching the patient suffer, not from pain, because we can stop or at least dull their pain, but watching the patient suffer a little more each day as they lose the ability to do one more thing for themselves. The family member may be angry because their loved one is dying or has recently died. Maybe they had to bear the burden of caring for their loved one because they never received any support from other family members. Their anger may actually be the fear they are feeling about their own uncertain future since for the past three years, they haven't done anything else but take care of their sick family member, and now they don't know how they are going to live without their loved one. Once the patient has died, the caregiver may no longer have a place to live or any means of financial support.

Or, their anger may be a result of the guilt they are feeling for having stayed away for years, or only rarely helped out. If so, they often overreact and lash out with anguish or anger at everyone around. I have witnessed family members getting hysterical over the dead body, throwing themselves on the floor, or punching the walls. These actions are often substitutions for the guilt they are feeling for not having been more involved or helpful. These actions help them process their guilt.

It is important for the hospice nurse to find a private space where she can sit down with family members when they are ready to talk and share their feelings. This must be a place where there won't be any interruptions. Now is the time to give your undivided attention and look the person in the eyes. Never interrupt when they are speaking. Follow their lead. Be empathetic. Never say anything that may minimize their feelings. Remember to call in other team members such as the social worker or chaplain to participate in the conversation or take over if necessary.

Always remember that listening and hearing are two different things. If you want to be a good hospice nurse and honestly communicate with others, use your intellect and your heart, and sincere communication will surely occur.

Attending so many different deaths, and taking care of so many kinds of patients and their families during the twelve years I have worked in hospice, has influenced the way I look at the world, the decisions I make, and the way I see the different neighborhoods and buildings in the Chicagoland area. I know I am a really good hospice nurse. Since the beginning of my career in hospice I have worked with hundreds of families. In some cases, I spend weeks and months with a family and build meaningful relationships with them. In other cases I have been invited into their lives for the briefest of moments.

I know I've made a difference in their lives. I hope they know how much they have influenced mine.

THE END